SOULUTIONS

A COLLECTION OF QUOTES TO INSPIRE

LUANNE PENNESI

To Grace,
Enjoy!
Luanne Pennesi

Soulutions: a collection of quotes to inspire
©Luanne Pennesi, 2008

ISBN 978-1-935110-00-2

Dedicated to my father,

B. Arthur Pennesi

Who provided me with love,
laughter, hope and unshakable
integrity throughout his entire life.

Acknowledgements

I would like to thank all of the inspiring authors of every timeless quote contained in this book. Your words will serve all of those willing to open their hearts and minds to their highest potential.

I also want to thank my family for supporting me through all of my work, whether they understand it or not. That is the root of unconditional love in my opinion.

Luanne Pennesi

Introduction

In a time when there is so much uncertainty and change happening all around us, we seek direction, understanding and comfort. There is nothing more inspiring than to open a book and find just the right words to help you through a particularly tough moment in your life, or to use someone else's words to help you to articulate a thought or concept more concisely.

There are many books of quotes. As a professional public speaker, consultant and vulnerable human being I have been drawn to the words of those who have the knowledge, passion and philosophy to validate my point or embellish a concept. For this I feel blessed.

These are the quotes that have touched my soul and lightened my heart. I am certain that several more editions (or "additions") will follow this collection.

Please sit back and enjoy this compilation of passages, poems, songs, quotes and sayings that may just be the thing you need to help you discover and appreciate the gift in this day.

For all the times I have searched for the right words and found someone already had them written out for me, I am grateful. I hope you find them as valuable as I have.

I invite feedback and additional quotes to add to future publications. Enjoy!

www.metropolitanwellness.com
whnn@aol.com

The way I see it,
if you want the rainbow,
you gotta put up with the rain.

Dolly Parton
(1946-)
Grammy-winning and Academy Award-
nominated American singer, songwriter,
composer, musician, author, and actress.

I t is not the critic who counts, nor the man who points out how the strong man stumbles or where the doer of deeds could have done them better. The credit belongs to the man who is actually in the arena, whose face is marred by dust and sweat and blood, who strives valiantly, who errs and comes up short again and again because there is no effort without error and shortcomings, who knows the great devotion, who spends himself in a worthy cause, who at the best knows in the end the high achievement of triumph and who at worst, if he fails while daring greatly, knows his place shall never be with those timid and cold souls who know neither victory nor defeat.

Theodore Roosevelt

(1858-1919)
26th President of the United States

*Good enough
never is.*

Debbi Fields
(1957-)
Founder, Mrs. Fields Cookies

Anyone can become angry—that is easy. But to be angry with the right person, to the right degree, at the right time, for the right purpose, and in the right way—that is not easy.

The Nichomachean Ethics

Aristotle

(384-322 BC)

Greek philosopher

Great dancers are not great because of their technique; they are great because of their passion.

Martha Graham

(1894-1991)
Choreographer, Founder of Modern Dance

5

The secret of getting ahead is getting started. The secret of getting started is breaking your complex overwhelming tasks into small manageable tasks, and then starting on the first one.

Samuel Langhorne Clemens

"*Mark Twain*"
(1835-1910)
American humorist, satirist, lecturer and writer

6

THE SIX MISTAKES
OF MAN

1. The delusion that personal gain is made by crushing others.

2. The tendency to worry about things that cannot be changed or corrected.

3. Insisting that a thing is impossible because we cannot accomplish it.

4. Refusing to set aside trivial preferences.

5. Neglecting development and refinement of the mind, and not acquiring the habit of reading and studying.

6. Attempting to compel others to believe and live as we do.

Marcus Tullius Cicero
(106-43 BC)
Roman statesman, lawyer, political
theorist, and philosopher.

7

In his *Creed for Optimists*, Christian D. Larsen tells you how you can be somebody.

Be so strong that nothing can disturb your peace of mind.

Talk health, happiness, and prosperity to every person you meet.

Make all your friends feel there is something special about them.

Look at the sunny side of everything.

Think only of the best, work only for the best, and expect only the best.

Be as enthusiastic about the success of others as you are about your own.

Forget the mistakes of the past and press on to the greater achievements of the future.

Give everyone a smile.

Spend so much time improving yourself that you have no time left to criticize others.

Be too big for worry and too noble for anger.

Be the change you want to see in the world.

Mohandas Gandhi

(1869-1948)
One of the most respected spiritual and
political leaders of the 1900s.

9

IF YOU HEAR A VOICE
WITHIN YOU SAYING "YOU
ARE NOT A PAINTER," THEN
BY ALL MEANS PAINT . . .
AND THAT VOICE WILL BE
SILENCED.

Vincent Van Gogh
(1853-1890)
Dutch Post-Impressionist artist

The significant problems we face today cannot be solved at the same level of thinking we were at when we created them.

Albert Einstein

(1879-1955)

Theoretical Physicist

A consultant is a man who knows 175 ways to make love, but doesn't know any women.

Sydney J. Harris

(1917-1985)
Journalist

You can't build a reputation
on what you're going
to do.

Henry Ford

(1863-1974)
Founder of the Ford Motor Company

Being responsible
sometimes means
pissing people off.

General Colin Powell
(1937-)
Soldier & Statesman

**Our chief want in life is
someone who shall make us do
what we can.**

*Ralph Waldo
Emerson*

(1803-1882)
American essayist, poet, and leader of the
Transcendentalist movement
in the early 19th century.

*B*e more concerned with your character than your reputation, because your character is what you really are, while your reputation is merely what others think you are.

John Wooden
(1910-)
Widely regarded as the greatest college basketball coach in history, with ten
NCAA National Championships.

16

Facts do not cease to be facts because they are ignored.

Aldous Huxley

(1894-1963)
British Author

B lame is the neat little device that you can use whenever you don't want to take responsibility for something in your life. Use it and you will avoid all risks and impede your own growth.

Wayne Dyer

(1940-)
American self-help advocate,
author and lecturer.

18

You change for two reasons:
you learn enough
and you want to or
you hurt enough
and you have to.

Randall Worley
Clergyman

Insanity is doing the same things over and over again, and expecting different results.

Albert Einstein

(1879-1955)

Theoretical Physicist and Nobel Laureate

Life is hard.
Easy is not an option.

Les Brown
(1945-)
Motivational speaker

Successful people are just
ordinary people who have
developed belief in themselves.

Dr. David Schwartz
Educator and Author

22

What man actually needs is not a tensionless state but rather the striving and struggling for some goal worthy of him. What he needs is not the discharge of tension at any cost, but the call of a potential meaning waiting to be fulfilled by him.

Victor Emil Frankl
(1905-1997)
Austrian neurologist and psychiatrist.

A ship in a safe harbor is safe, but that is not what a ship is built for.

William Greenough Thayer Shedd

(1820-1894)
Considered one of the greatest systematic
theologians of the American Presbyterian Church.

You were born
an original.
Don't die a copy.

John Mason

A kiss is a lovely trick
designed by nature
to stop speech when words
become superfluous.

Ingrid Bergman

(1915-1982)
Academy, Emmy and Tony Award-winning
Swedish actress.

You've got to get to the stage
in life where going for it is
more important than winning
or losing.

Arthur Ashe
(1943-1993)
Tennis champion.

Only those who risk going too far will ever know how far they can go.

Unkown Author

A successful man is one who
can build a firm foundation
with the bricks that others
throw at him.

David Brinkley

(1920-2003)
Television journalist, commentator
and author.

Success seems to be largely a matter of hanging on after others have let go.

William Feather

(1889-1981)
American publisher and author.

If you live to be a hundred, I want to live to be a hundred minus one day, so I never have to live without you.

Winnie the Pooh
A.A. Milne
(1882-1956)
English author

We all take different paths in
life, but no matter where we go,
we take a little of each other
everywhere.

Tim McGraw
(1967-)
American country music singer

Never hit a man with glasses.
Hit him with something
bigger and heavier.

Anonymous

Aerodynamically
the bumblebee shouldn't
be able to fly,
but the bumblebee doesn't know
so it goes on flying anyway.

Mary Kay Ash

(1918-2001)
U.S. businesswoman and founder of
Mary Kay Cosmetics.

After winter comes the summer. After night comes the dawn. And after every storm, there comes clear, open skies.

Samuel Rutherford

(1600-1661)
Scottish pastor

Dream big dreams, then put on
your overalls and go out and
make the dreams come true.

Fred Van Amburgh

TO KNOW AND
NOT TO DO,
IS NOT YET TO KNOW.

ZEN PROVERB

37

The only thing we have to fear is fear itself—nameless, unreasoning, unjustified terror which paralyzes needed efforts to convert retreat into advance.

Franklin Delano Roosevelt

(1882-1945)
32nd President of the United States

You gain strength, courage and confidence by every experience in which you really stop to look fear in the face . . . You must do the thing you think you cannot do.

Eleanor Roosevelt

(1884-1962)
Wife of 32nd U.S. President
and human rights activist.

The tragedy of life doesn't lie in not reaching your goal. The tragedy lies in having no goal to reach.

Benjamin Mays
(1895–1984)
African-American minister, educator, scholar, social activist and the president of Morehouse College in Atlanta, Georgia.

W hen you get into a tight
place and everything goes
against you til it seems as though
you could not hold on a minute
longer, never give up then, for that
is just the place and time that the
tide will turn.

Harriet Beecher Stowe
(1811-1896)
American abolitionist and novelist.

41

It is not by accident that the happiest people are those who make a conscious effort to live useful lives. Their happiness, of course, is not a shallow exhilaration where life is one continuous intoxicating party. Rather, their happiness is a deep sense of inner peace that comes when they believe their lives have meaning and that they are making a difference for good in the world.

Ernest A. Fitzgerald
(1925-)
American Bishop of the
United Methodist Church

Energy and persistence
conquer all things.

Benjamin Franklin
(1706-1790)
Author, political theorist, politician, printer,
scientist, inventor, civic activist, and diplomat.

How is it possible that a being with such sensitive jewels as the eyes, such enchanted musical instruments as the ears, and such fabulous arabesque of nerves as the brain can experience itself be anything less than a god.

Alan Watts
(1915–1973)
Philosopher, author, speaker.

People who do not succeed have one distinguishing trait in common. They know all the reasons for failure and have what they believe to be airtight alibis to explain their own lack of achievement.

Napoleon Hill
(1883-1970)
American author and one of the
earliest producers of personal-success literature.
His most famous work, *Think and Grow Rich*.

I get satisfaction of three kinds.
One is creating something,
one is being paid for it, and
one is the feeling that I haven't
just been sitting on my ass all
afternoon.

William F. Buckley

(1925-2008)
American author and
conservative commentator.

*One's feelings waste
themselves in words; they ought
all to be distilled into action...
which brings results.*

Florence Nightingale

(1820-1910)
Pioneer of modern nursing.

I make all my decisions on intuition. I throw a spear into the darkness. That is intuition. Then I must send an army into the darkness to find the spear. That is intellect.

Ingmar Bergman

(1918-2007)
Swedish film, stage, and opera director,
widely revered as one of the
greatest filmmakers of the 20th century.

The more I give myself permission
to live in the moment
and enjoy it without feeling guilty
or judgemental about any other time,
the better I feel
about the quality of my work.

Wayne Dyer
(1940-)
American self-help advocate,
author and lecture

The "control of nature" is a phrase conceived in arrogance, born of the Neanderthal age of biology and the convenience of man.

Rachel Carson

(1907-1964)
American marine biologist and
nature writer.

50

Vacillating people seldom succeed. They seldom win the solid respect of their fellows. Successful men and women are very careful in reaching decisions, and very persistent and determined in action thereafter.

L.G. Elliott

No matter how big and tough a problem may be, get rid of confusion by taking one little step towards solution. Do something. Then try again. At the worst, so long as you don't do it the same way twice, you will eventually use up all the wrong ways of doing it and thus the next try will be the right one.

George F. Nordenholt

It is the greatest shot of adrenaline to be doing what you've wanted to do so badly. You almost feel like you could fly without the plane.

Charles Lindbergh
(1902-1974)
Adventurer and explorer.

The road to happiness lies in two simple principals: find what it is that interests you and that you can do well, and when you find it put your whole soul into it – every bit of energy and ambition and natural ability you have.

John D. Rockefeller

(1839–1937)
American industrialist.

To think is easy.
To act is difficult.
To act as one thinks
is the most difficult at all.

Johann von Goethe
(1749-1832)
German author.

The world has a way of giving what is demanded of it. If you are frightened and look for failure and poverty, you will get them, no matter how hard you may try to succeed. Lack of faith in yourself, in what life will do for you, cuts you off from the good things in the world. Expect victory and you make victory. Nowhere is this truer than in business life, where bravery and faith bring both material and spiritual rewards.

Preston Bradley

Minister

56

You must understand the whole of life, not just one little part of it. That is why you must read, that is why you must look at the skies, that is why you must sing, and dance, and write poems, and suffer, and understand, for all that is life.

Jiddu Krishnamurti

(1895–1986)
Writer and speaker on
philosophical and spiritual subjects.

T here is a very real relationship, both quantitatively and qualitatively, between what you contribute and what you get out of this world.

Oscar Hammerstein III
(1847-1919)
Inventor, writer, editor, publisher, composer, designer, builder, promoter, showman.

I THINK THE PURPOSE OF LIFE IS TO BE USEFUL, TO BE RESPONSIBLE, TO BE HONORABLE, TO BE COMPASSIONATE. IT IS, AFTER ALL, TO MATTER: TO COUNT, TO STAND FOR SOMETHING, TO HAVE MADE SOME DIFFERENCE THAT YOU LIVED AT ALL.

Leo C. Rosten

(1908-1997)
Teacher, academic, screenwriter
and humorist.

The battle of life is, in most cases, fought uphill; and to win it without a struggle were perhaps to win it without honor. If there were no difficulties there would be no success; if there were nothing to struggle for, there would be nothing to be achieved.

Samuel Smiles
(1812-1904)
Scottish author and reformer

There are but two roads that lead to an important goal and to the doing of great things: strength and perseverance. Strength is the lot of but a few privileged men; but austere perseverance, harsh and continuous, may be employed by the smallest of us and rarely fails of its purpose, for its silent power grows irresistibly greater with time.

Johann van Goethe
(1749-1832)
German author.

Take your life in your own hands, and what happens? A terrible thing: no one to blame.

Erica Jong

(1942-)
American author.

Strength does not come from winning. Your struggles develop your strengths.

When you go through hardships and decide not to surrender, that is strength.

Arnold Schwarzenegger
(1947-)
Austrian-American bodybuilder,
actor, and politician

63

Without ambition one starts nothing. Without work one finishes nothing. The prize will not be sent to you. As to methods there may be a million and then some, but the principles are few. The man who grasps principles can successfully select his own methods. The man who tries methods, ignoring principles, is sure to have trouble.

Ralph Waldo Emerson
(1803-1882)
American essayist, poet, and leader of the
Transcendentalist movement
in the early 19th century.

The successful person is the individual who forms the habit of doing what the failing person doesn't like to do.

Donald Riggs

When one door of happiness closes, another opens; but often we look so long at the closed door that we do not see the one that has been opened for us.

Helen Keller

(1880-1968)
Deafblind American author,
activist and lecturer.

The imagination is the
workshop of the soul, where
are shaped all the plans for
individual achievement.

Napoleon Hill

(1883-1970)
American author and one of the
earliest producers of personal-success literature.

In the face of uncertainty,
there is nothing wrong
with hope.

Bernie S. Siegel, M.D.

Doctor involved in humanizing
medical education.

**Dare to receive a drop and in time
you'll be given the ocean.**

MasterPath
A form of spiritual practice that is
followed in the Sant Mat.

We are all assigned a piece of the garden, a corner of the universe that is ours to transform. Our corner of the universe is our own life—our relationships, our homes, our work, our current circumstances—exactly as they are.

Marianne Williamson
(1952-)
Spiritual activist, author, lecturer and
founder of The Peace Alliance.

Progress always involves
risk;
you can't steal second base
and keep your foot on first.

Anonymous

Bless those who challenge us to grow, to stretch, to move beyond the knowable, to come back home to our elemental and essential nature. Bless those who challenge us for they remind us of doors we have closed and doors we have yet to open.

Navajo saying

The future is simply infinite possibility waiting to happen. What it waits on is human imagination to crystallize its possibility.

Leland Kaiser
Futurist and motivational speaker.

The woods would be a very
silent place if no birds sang
except those who sang best.

Bernard Meltzer
(1917-1998)
Radio host.

You can explore the universe looking for somebody who is more deserving of your love and affection than you are, and you will not find that person anywhere.

Buddhist Expression

Our thoughts,
without reservation,
tend to make us sick or healthy.

Deepak Chopra

(1946-)
Indian medical doctor and writer.

On the road to life
you only have one
companion. Learn to
be good company to
yourself.

Nellie Lincoln

**Nothing is quite as funny
as the unintended humor of reality.**

Steve Allen
(1921-2000)
American musician, comedian, writer and
television personality.

78

We all have wings,
but some don't know why...

sung by INXS

To break free is to go beyond into the unknown that is speculative, conjecture, uncertain. And out there, entity, you have all the freedom to take, for the first time in your existence, your own God-given brilliance, that you certainly are, and apply it in a way that you deliver yourself from the enslavement of someone else's ideals and create your own.

Ramtha

The central figure (the "master teacher")
of Ramtha's School of Enlightenment (RSE), a
school started by JZ Knight in 1987
in Yelm, Washington.

If you follow your bliss, you put yourself on a kind of track that has been there all the while waiting for you, and the life you ought to be living is the one you are living. When you can see that, you begin to meet people who are in the field of your bliss, and they open the doors to you. I say, follow your bliss and don't be afraid, and doors will open where you didn't know they were going to be. If you follow your bliss, doors will open for you that wouldn't have opened for anyone else.

Joseph Campbell

(1904-1987)
American mythology professor and writer
best known for his work in the fields of
comparative mythology and comparative religion.

Poor is the man whose pleasure depends on the permission of another.

Madonna
(1958-)
American dance-pop singer-songwriter,
dancer, record, film producer, actress.

Too much of a good thing
can be wonderful.

Mae West

(1893-1980)
American actress, playwright, screenwriter,
and sex symbol.

The day will happen whether or not you get up.

John Ciardi

(1916-1986)
American poet, translator,
and etymologist

He's turned his life around.
He used to be depressed
and miserable. Now he's
miserable and depressed.

David Frost
(1939-)
English television personality.

**Blessed are the sleepy,
for they shall soon drop off.**

Friedrich Nietzsche
(1844-1900)
19th century German philosopher.

Lost wealth may be replaced by industry,

lost knowledge by study,

lost health by temperance or medicine,

but lost time is gone forever.

Samuel Smiles
(1812-1904)
Scottish author and reformer

*When choosing
between two evils,
I always like to
try the one I've
never tried before.*

Mae West
(1893-1980)
American actress, playwright, screenwriter,
and sex symbol.

88

No matter where you are in life, no matter what you've contributed to creating, no matter what's happening, you are always doing the best you can with the understanding and awareness and knowledge that you have.

Louise L. Hay

Motivational speaker; one of the founders of the self-help movement.

Remind thyself, in the darkest moments, that every failure is only a step toward success, every detection of what is false directs you toward what is true, every trial exhausts some tempting form of error, and every adversity will only hide, for a time, your path to peace and fulfillment.

Og Mandina
(1923-1996)
American motivational author, speaker.

"**Always**" is never true; reality isn't a vast fixed scheme trapping you without choice. At any moment you have the choice to break out of what is really trapping you – your automatic reactions dredged up from the past.

Deepak Chopra

(1946-)
Indian medical doctor and writer.

Obstacles are those frightful things you see when you take your eyes off the goal.

Hannah More
(1745-1833)
English religious writer and philanthropist.

It makes no difference how deeply seated may be the trouble, how hopeless the outlook, how muddled the tangle, how great the mistake. A sufficient realization of love will dissolve it all.

Emmet Fox
(1886-1951)
New Thought spiritual leader of the
early 20th Century

For a long time it had seemed to me that life was about to begin—real life. But there was always some obstacle in the way. Something to be got through first, some unfinished business, time still to be served, a debt to be paid. Then life would begin. At last it dawned on me that these obstacles were my life.

Fr. Alfred D´Souza

Enlightenment is seeing that the world you've created inside your head doesn't really exist, except as a fabrication in your mind.

Jim Dreaver

Author of *The Way of Harmony.*

W e look at some people as if they were special, gifted, divine. Nobody is special and gifted and divine. No more than you are, no more than I am. The only difference, the very only one, is that they have begun to understand what they really are and have begun to practice it.

Richard Bach

Author of *Illusions: The Adventures of a Reluctant Messiah.*

When I despair, I remember that all through history the way of truth and love has always won. There have been tyrants and murderers and for a time they seem invincible but in the end, they always fall —think of it, ALWAYS.

Mohandas Gandhi

(1869-1948)
Indian political activist famous for doctrine of "passive resistance."

To be yourself in a world
that is constantly trying
to make you something
else is the greatest
accomplishment.

Ralph Waldo Emerson
(1803-1882)
American essayist, poet, and leader of the
Transcendentalist movement
in the early 19th century.

Nobody grows old merely by living a number of years. We grow old by deserting our ideals. Years may wrinkle the skin, but to give up enthusiasm wrinkles the soul.

Samuel Ullman
(1840-1924)
American businessman, poet,
humanitarian.

The sun emits no fear of ever running out of light. The moon reflects no fear of darkness in the cool of night. Trees are not afraid of losing some or all of their leaves, trusting in the flow of nature's generosity. Ants do not obsess about the things they have to do. Eagles don't concern themselves with running out of food. The ocean gives itself to sky, no fear of running dry – Why is it then that I'm afraid? How different am I?

Lion Goodman
Entrepreneur, author, teacher.

All truth goes through three steps: First, it is ridiculed. Second, it is violently opposed. Finally, it is accepted as self-evident.

Arthur Schopenhauer

(1788-1860)
German philosopher.

Death comes to all,
but great achievements
build a monument which
shall endure until the sun
grows cold.

George Fabricius

Learn how to love people and use things—not love things and use people.

n how to love people and

use *Gary Null*

(1945-)

Talk radio host and author on alternative and complementary medicine and nutrition.

If you want total security, go to prison. There you're fed, clothed, and given medical care and so on. The only thing lacking . . . is freedom.

Dwight D. Eisenhower
(1890-1969)
Five-star General who became the
34th President of the United States.

The one law that does not change is that everything changes, and the hardship I was bearing today was only a breath away from the pleasures I would have tomorrow, and those pleasures would be all the richer because of the memories of this I was enduring.

Louis L'Amour
(1908-1988)
Bestselling American author of
Western fiction.

We are continually faced by great opportunities brilliantly disguised as insoluble problems.

Lee Iacocca
(1924-)
American industrialist.

I've never met a person, I don't care what his condition, in whom I could not see possibilities. I don't care how much a man may consider himself a failure, I believe in him, for he can change the thing that is wrong in his life anytime he is prepared and ready to do it. Whenever he develops the desire, he can take away from his life the thing that is defeating it. The capacity for reformation and change lies within.

Preston Bradley
Minister

Character cannot be developed in ease and quiet. Only through experience of trial and suffering can the soul be strengthened, vision cleared, ambition inspired, and success achieved.

Helen Keller

(1880-1968)
Deafblind American author,
activist and lecturer.

If you don't make a total commitment to whatever you're doing, then you start looking to bail out the first time the boat stars leaking. It's tough enough getting that boat to shore with everybody rowing, let alone when a guy stands up and starts putting his life jacket on.

Lou Holtz

(1937-)
Author, television commentator, motivational speaker, and former NCAA football coach.

Go to the place where the thing you wish to know is native; your best teacher is there ... You acquire a language most readily in the country where it is spoken, you study mineralogy best among miners, and so with everything else.

Johann von Goethe
(1749-1832)
German author.

*I am a great believer in
luck, and I find the harder
I work, the more
I have of it.*

Thomas Jefferson

(1743-1826)
3rd President of the United States
and principal author of the
Declaration of Independence (1776).

*L*ife is not governed by will or intention. Life is a question of nerves, and fibers, and slowly built-up cells in which thought hides itself, and passion has its dreams.

Oscar Wilde
(1854-1900)
Irish playwright, novelist, poet.

Courage is being scared to death ...and saddling up anyway.

John Wayne

(1907-1979)
Academy Award-winning film actor
and American icon.

113

Nothing can stop the man with the right mental attitude from achieving his goal; nothing on earth can help the man with the wrong mental attitude.

W.W. Ziege

*Use your health, even
to the point of wearing
it out. That is what it is
for. Spend all you have
before you die; do not
outlive yourself.*

George Bernard Shaw
(1856-1950)
World-renowned Irish author.

In this time of exponential growth, if you can sustain and expand success, you can be ripe and ready to seize the moment that can catapult your success and happiness beyond the limits of your imagination and belief. If you cannot sustain and expand success, you are at risk and in jeopardy of losing it.

Lazaris

A channeled nonphysical entity
created by Jach Pursel.

Success is not
counted by how
high you have climbed
but by how many
people you brought
with you.

Wil Rose

We travel together as passengers on a little spaceship, dependent on its vulnerable reserves of air and soil; all committed for our safety to its security and peace; preserved from annihilation only by the care, the work, and I'll say the love we give our fragile craft. We cannot maintain it half-fortunate, half-miserable, half-confident, half-despairing, half-slave to the ancient enemies of man, half-free in liberation of resources undreamed of until this day. No craft, no crew can travel safely with such contradictions. On their resolution depends the survival of us all.

Adlai Stevenson

(1900-1965)

American politician and statesman.

All mankind is divided into
three classes:
those that are immovable,
those that are movable,
and those that move.

Benjamin Franklin
(1706-1790)
American scientist, publisher and diplomat.

When you adopt the viewpoint that there is nothing that exists that is not part of you, that there is no one who exists that is not part of you, that any judgment you make is self-judgment, that any criticism you level is self-criticism, you will wisely extend to yourself an unconditional love that will be the light of your world.

Harry Palmer

Author of *The Avatar Materials.*

The trouble with many of us is that we just slide along in life. If we would only give, just once, the same amount of reflection to what we want out of life that we give to the question of what to do with a two-week vacation, we would be startled at our false standards and the aimless procession of our busy days.

Dorothy Canfield Fisher
(1879-1958)
American writer.

121

W

e can throw stones,
complain about them,
stumble on them,
climb over them,
or build with them.

William Arthur
Ward
(1921 – 1994)
Author of *Fountains of Faith*.

It is not the load that
breaks you down,
it's the way you carry it.

Lena Horne
(1917-)
Singer and actress.

One man cannot do right in one department of life whilst he is occupied doing wrong in any other department. Life is one indivisible whole.

Mohandas Gandhi

(1869-1948)
Indian spiritual and political leader.

To know what you prefer, instead of humbly saying "Amen" to what the world tells you you ought to prefer, is to keep your soul alive.

Robert Louis Stevenson

(1850-1894)
Scottish novelist, poet, and
travel writer.

Up to a point a man's life is shaped by environment, heredity, and movements and changes in the world about him; then there comes a time when it lies within his grasp to shape the clay of his life into the sort of thing he wishes to be... Everyone has it within his power to say, this I am today, that I shall be tomorrow.

Louis L' Amour
(1908-1988)
American author of
Western fiction.

126

The greatest good you can do
for another is not just to share
your riches,
but to reveal to him his own.

Benjamin Disraeli
(1804-1881)
British Conservative statesman and author who
served twice as prime minister.

Procrastination is opportunity's assassin.

Victor Kiam

(1926-2001)
American entrepreneur.

I count him braver who overcomes his desires than him who conquers his enemies; the hardest victory is the victory over self.

Aristotle
(384-322 BC)
Greek philosopher.

Success is going from failure to failure without loss of enthusiasm.

Sir Winston Churchill
(1874-1965)
British politician who served twice
as prime minister.

So what do we do? Anything. Something. So long as we don't sit there. If we screw it up, start over. Try something else. If we wait until we satisfied all the uncertainties, it may be too late.

Lee Iacocca
(1924-)
American industrialist.

Knowledge is power, but
enthusiasm pulls the switch.

Ivern Ball

Defeat is a state of mind. No one is ever defeated until defeat has been accepted as a reality. To me, defeat in anything is merely temporary, and its punishment is but an urge for me to greater effort to achieve my goal. Defeat simply tells me that something is wrong in my doing; it is a path leading to success and truth.

Bruce Lee
(1940-1973)
Chinese-American martial artist,
actor, director, author.

We either make
ourselves miserable,
or we make ourselves
strong. The amount of
work is the same.

Carlos Castaneda

(1925-1998)
American author.

How To Be Really Alive!

Live juicy. Stamp out conformity. Stay in bed all day. Dream of gypsy wagons. Find snails making love. Develop an astounding appetite for books. Drink sunsets. Draw out your feelings. Amaze yourself. Be ridiculous. Stop worrying now. If not now, then when? Make yes your favorite word. Marry yourself. Dry your clothes in the sun. Eat mangoes naked. Keep toys in the bathtub. Spin yourself dizzy. Hang upside down. Follow a child. Celebrate an old person. Send a love letter to yourself. Be advanced. Try endearing. Invent new ways to love. Transform negatives. Delight someone. Wear pajamas to a drive-in movie. Allow yourself to feel rich without money. Be who you truly are and the money will follow. Believe in everything. You are always on your way to a miracle.

THE MIRACLE IS YOU

Sark

Consciousness is a great privilege. But consciousness is also an obligation, the obligation to live in ever deepening relationship. The on-going invitation of life is to go beyond the threshold of our fears, beyond the boundaries of who or what we think we are. Instead of living from our smaller, contracted self which in seeking for security chooses to remain separate, we are forever being invited into our larger self which is already in profound relationship with all that is.

Dr. Richard Moss

Thinker, teacher and author of books on transformation, self-healing and the art of conscious living.

If you hang around achievers, you will be a better achiever; hang around givers and you will be a better giver; hang around thinkers and you will be a better thinker; but, hang around a bunch of thumb-sucking complaining boneheads, and you will be a better thumb-sucking complaining bonehead.

Charles Jones

Oscar Wilde said, "Consistency is the last refuge of the imaginative." So stop getting up at 6:05. Get up at 5:06. Walk a mile at dawn. Find a new way to drive to work. Switch chores with your spouse next Saturday. Buy a wok. Study wildflowers. Stay up alone all night. Read to the blind. Start counting brown-eyed blondes or blonds. Subscribe to an out-of-town paper. Canoe at midnight. Don't write to your senator, take a whole scout troop to see her. Learn to speak Italian. Teach some kid the thing you do best. Listen to two hours of uninterrupted Mozart. Take up calligraphy. Leap out of that rut. Savor life. Remember, we only pass this way once.

Author unknown

**Don't be afraid to take
a big step when one is
indicated. You can't cross
a chasm in two small steps.**

David Lloyd George

(1863-1945)
British statesman and
prime minister.

ever compromise a dream. Do what you must. The fears, beasts, and mountains before you are part of the plan. Stepping stones to a promised land. To a time and place that is so much closer than even you expect. So don't let your eyes deceive you, for even as you read these words, your ship swiftly approaches.

Michael Dooley
author of *Infinite Possibilities -
The Art of Living Your Dreams.*

The very greatest things—
great thoughts, discoveries,
inventions—have usually
been nurtured in hardship,
often pondered over in
sorrow, and at length
established with difficulty.

Samuel Smiles
(1812-1904)
Scottish author and reformer.

When you're following your energy and doing what you want all the distinction between work and play dissolves.

Shakti Gawain

Pioneer in the field of personal development.

The beliefs you truly hold, the ones you've decided to believe, your faith will cause you to create or attract the experiences which will verify them. When you change your beliefs, your experiences will change.

Harry Palmer
Author

Coincidences
are God's way
of remaining
anonymous.

Author Unknown

S ometimes life is like a roller coaster, when you'd really rather be on the Ferris wheel. When you feel that big drop coming hold on, enjoy the ride, and remember that life is a great adventure.

Heidi Listug

Each relationship you have with another person reflects the relationship you have with yourself.

Alice Denille

Positive, continuous action toward your goals is the very best antidote to worry.

Brian Tracy
(1944-)
Self-help author.

Act the way you want to be
and soon you will be the way
you act.

Dr. Johnnie Coleman

You are not here merely to make a living. You are here in order to enable the world to live more amply, with greater vision, with a finer spirit of hope and achievement. You are here to enrich the world and you impoverish yourself if you forget the errand.

Woodrow Wilson
(1856-1924)
28th President of the United States.

Life is raw material.
We are artisans.
We can sculpt our existence
into something beautiful,
or debase it into ugliness.
It's in our hands.

Cathy Better

150

Bless those who challenge us to grow, to stretch, to move beyond the knowable, to come back home to our elemental and essential nature. Bless those who challenge us for they remind us of doors we have closed and doors we have yet to open.

Navajo saying

151

Life is either a daring adventure or nothing.

Helen Keller

(1880-1968)
Deafblind American author,
activist and lecturer.

**The difference between
a successful person and
others is not a lack of
strength,
not a lack of knowledge,
but rather in a lack of will.**

Vince Lombardi
(1913-1970)
One of the most successful coaches in the history
of American football,
winning five NFL championships.

Doubters do not achieve.
Skeptics do not contribute.
Cynics do not create.

Calvin Coolidge

(1872-1933)
30th President of the United States.

There is no one else like you
on the planet. There never
has been and there never will
be. You are forever a unique,
divine creation.

Louise L. Hay
Motivational speaker, one of the founders
of the self-help movement.

You can't have a fear of
dying until you first have a
fear of living.

Gary Null

From Brian Tracy's
Success Strategies:
6 Requirements for Being Successful

1.   Peace of mind; freedom from fear, anger & guilt
2.   High levels of health and energy
3. Loving relationships
4. Financial freedom
5. Worthy goals and ideals
6. A feeling of personal fulfillment; that we are becoming everything that we are capable of becoming as a human being.

COME TO THE EDGE
LIFE SAID.
THEY SAID:
WE ARE AFRAID.
COME TO THE EDGE
LIFE SAID.
THEY CAME.
IT PUSHED THEM . . .
AND THEY FLEW.

Guillaume
Apollinaire
(1880-1918)
French poet, writer, and art critic.

When we think of the "price" of success, we think of what we must give up or give in exchange for the benefits that succeeding brings. We think of the bargain we must strike or the compromise we must make to have greater success.

Often we don't even explore the possibility of uncompromising success. Even more, we do not consider the magic of a price that is without compromise.

Lazaris

M oderation? It's mediocrity, fear, and confusion in disguise. It's the devil's dilemma. It's neither doing nor not doing. It's the wobbling compromises that makes no one happy. Moderation is for the bland, the apologetic, for the fence-sitters of the world afraid to take a stand. It's for those afraid to laugh or cry, for those afraid to live or die. Moderation . . . is lukewarm tea, the devil's own brew.

Dan Millman
author, *Way Of The Peaceful Warrior*

160

Truth lives on in the midst of deception.

Johann Friedrich von Schiller

(1759-1805)
German poet, philosopher,
historian, and dramatist.

Three things in human life are
important. The first is to be kind.
The second is to be kind. And
the third is to be kind.

Henry James

to his nephew, William James
as quoted in Leon Edel's *Henry James: A Life.*

162

Our deepest fear is not that we are inadequate.

Our deepest fear is that we are powerful beyond measure.

It is our light not our darkness that most frightens us.

We ask ourselves, who am I to be brilliant, gorgeous, talented and fabulous?

Actually, who are you not to be?

You are a child of God.

Your playing small doesn't serve the world.

There's nothing enlightened about shrinking so that other people won't feel insecure around you.

We were born to make manifest the glory of God that is within us.

It's not just in some of us; it's in everyone.

And as we let our own light shine, we unconsciously give other people permission to do the same.

As we are liberated from our own fear, our presence automatically liberates others.

Nelson Mandela

(1918-)

Anti-apartheid activtist and first democratically elected president of South Africa.

**Understanding your
mission is to make
history while you are here.**

The doctor of the future will give no medicine, but will interest patients in the care of the human frame, in diet, and in the cause and prevention of disease.

Thomas Edison

ABOUT THE AUTHOR

Luanne Pennesi, a registered nurse practicing for nearly 30 years in both conventional and integrative medicine, is a rising star in the field of natural health, sharing information that motivates people to take back their personal power and lead happier, more productive lives at ANY age.

Luanne is a dynamic, energizing individual who makes learning holistic health concepts fun and interesting.

Luanne has successfully reversed herpes, hepatitis, chronic fatigue syndrome, acne (and the pock marks that resulted from it), polycystic breast disease, cystic ovaries, PMS, menopause, chronic mycoplasma, pneumonia, restless leg syndrome, chronic yeast, nail fungus, severe myopia, hypothyroidism and addictions to caffeine and sugar.

Luanne lives the adventurous, authentic lifestyle she prescribes for others. She is a world-class athlete in race walking and roller skate ballroom dancing.